old soul love

Christopher Poindexter

Andrews McMeel
PUBLISHING®

Pragma

My grandmother
and grandfather
had the old soul love.
It was truly your hand in mine,
until the end of time.
I watched her hug him,
her aging arms
wrapped around his
barely breathing body as
he took his last breaths.
"Goodbye, Jack,
I'll never forget you."
I still find myself broken up
about that moment.
I wear his cologne
out everywhere I go.
I like to think I am
keeping him alive
a little longer for Grandma
in this way,
ordering his favorite tequila,
embodying
his gritty charisma.
I aim for this love.
It's somewhere out there,
and I know it.
I am in the small
and quiet army
of hopeful romantics.
The holding hands,
deathbed kind of love.

How could
I forget her?
First lovers
might as well
be a body part.
We will always
carry them.

It is impossible
to not be romantic
with the world
when we exist
beneath a sun
that constantly
makes love
to the horizon.

If I shall die
before her,
I beg of you,
whoever is in control—
God, cosmos,
nature, ocean—
give my body
to the sun
so that every time
it finds its way
to her flesh
she is never without
the warmth
of my love.

I watched a girl
in a sundress kiss
another girl on a park bench,
and just as the sunlight spilled
perfectly onto
their hair,
I thought to myself,
"How bravely beautiful it is,
that sometimes
the sea wants the city,
even
when it has been told its entire
life it was
meant for the shore."

I miss you
even when you are
beside me.
I dream
of your celestial body
even when you are
sleeping in my arms.
The words *I love you*
will never be enough.

I suppose
we'll have to invent
new ones.

He thought,
as the moonlight swam
into the window and lit her
shoulder blades,
"There is nothing more beautiful
than the way the universe is
always chasing you."

My dearest, I cannot express this to you
enough: there are not enough words
in any language to measure you up,
but I devote my life to doing the best
that I can, weaving and spinning through
gardens of poetry, trying to pluck
the dearest verses, the darling reason,
the highest sentiments, for you.
You are simply what you are, and you
exist in such perfection that forces me
to never turn away, my eyes always
pressed softly to the hue of you,
my body begging and yearning for more,
always more. You simply are.
You are the smell of rain and the way
it arouses my body in love; you are
the golden blood of jazz and the sexy, serene
sound of the sax sung to me whitely
in the morning; you are every street name
and sunrise and sunset I have missed
because I was in bed with you, too foolish
to leave but wise enough to stay and know
the difference; you are every stone
that has found a way to charm me, to drip
my beautiful blood blue into its energy;
you, my sweetness, are never without,
you are everywhere I go and all that I do,
it's you, always you;
you are everything, absolutely everything,
and the sea.

The universe
wrote fiction
in us;
it's called fear.

If there
is one thing
I have learned
in this world,
from observation,
from failure,
from struggling
to love
the only self
I will ever own,
it's that more
than anything
in this world
people these days
are so petrified,
so terribly petrified,
to just be natural.

There are pieces
in me
that die
when she leaves
these blankets.

I loved her
not for the way
she danced
with my angels but
for the way
the sound
of her name
could silence
my demons.

One
of the most flattering
things I have come to know
is when someone tells me,
"I am in love with the way
you see the world."

How sincerely beautiful
it is for someone to simply
say your eyes are art.

I grew up listening to
my father say my little brother's
name over and over and over
into his newborn ears until
he finally understood that
name was his own.
Now I am older, and some days
I find myself whispering into
your ears over and over and over,
"I love you, I love you,"
until you begin to understand
that I am truly yours.

confident
in one's own skin,
in the end,
all that truly
matters.

My grandfather told me
to never be on time;
it just shows you're
conforming and playing
by their rules.
He always said,
"There is nothing worse
than their rules, kid."
I remember him always,
in the smell of his cologne bottle
I reach for every morning,
in the lifeless, lost smile
now on my grandmother's
forgotten face.
If I could, I would trade my body for his.
Put me in the ground
and crown my grandmother again.
In foolish love she would
stare at him,
wide eyed and marvelous.
While I smile wildly
from the throat of my grave.

My dear future
I do not know you by name
not by gender
not by the sparkle in your earthy eyes
or the smoothness of your inner thighs
no, I do not
and I don't want to.
Who knows the man I will become
who knows the good I will do
the good I won't do
what I will or will not have the strength for
and what good is it to know?

All that matters is potential
and the double-barrel stare
to see it through.

What could be
more brave and
honorable than loving yourself
no matter the cost,
so that you can give that
love away to others
and become the change,
the difference?

And maybe
in the end,
we were all just humans,
drunk on the idea
that love,
only love,
could heal
our brokenness.

the answer
will always be found
in nature.
no matter the question.
I have found the people
with the biggest hearts
open themselves
up to it all—
sun and moon,
ocean and meadow,
gardens and birds,
trees and mountains.
the universe is always
trying to tell us something.
if only we would listen.

we become better people
when we do.

I want sex
so passionate
the stars
rip open the roof
of our bedroom
just to watch.

My aim is not only
to tell you I love you,
to not only
whisper sweet, lovely nothings
in your eager ears,
but rather to show you,
my clenched fist unfurling
out of its fearful, loveless past, my
heart open in celestial bloom, you
can have all of me.
Every inch of marrow and flesh.

I pushed away
love I felt I didn't deserve
courted poetry
down to the water
instead
in her white dress
wrapped her arms
around me
like the sound
of a piano breathing
poetry will never break you
I wrote into the stone
poetry will never die
I wrote again
poetry is not jealous
poetry just is
it stands alone
as this ancient thing
this way of talking
this way of being
this way of healing
when I die
bury me among the pages
I want my body
to be drenched
in all the words
I never said
but the ones that have always
existed inside me.

In the end,
when
our eyes
find their
infinite darkness,
you will know that
our bodies
were tiny universes,
and I love you
with a thousand seas.

There
are maps
through your bones
and skin,
to the way
you've felt,
and the way
you've been.

How truly
terrible it is
that those
who are silent
are often seen
as empty.

The root
of my heaviness
is quite simple:
so much to love,
so little time.

We softly
got lost
in the things
that would take
us away
and we never returned
from them again.
To us,
that was each other.

She buried
her ears in the calm
of his heartbeat,
and in a matter of seconds
fell terribly in love
with the way her loneliness
fell softly
and suddenly
asleep
in his chest.

It was the day I first saw you in that dress,
black and red roses enveloped over body,
your hair metallic and tossing as you twirled for me.
"Does it look good, baby?"
If only you knew. Often I am afraid to tell you.
But in my own ways, I do.
When spirit is just as beautiful as body,
and body as spirit, it does something to a man,
makes him question everything he has ever known,
sends him to, say, a blank page,
or a piano bench, or a canvas,
hungry to make poetic sense of it,
of the way it feels to look into
the almond eyes of a woman
and lose himself,
his ego hovering
and trembling above him,
his hands better things,
his heart an invitation.
I find myself on the white blank page often,
daydreaming to John Coltrane's saxophone
of that tender, romantic love
that exists in absolute rarity,
the kind that kisses both light and wound,
both flesh and soul,
and gives a man the courage
to go beyond himself,
to not listen to cock,
rather the water of being,
and take his woman
by the hands
and offer her the entire world.

I want my woman to taste my love,
truly taste it.

I want to drench her to the bone
in roses and poetry and kisses
and colors unknown.

Practice
forgiveness,
especially on
yourself.

I love our sun-diving hips,
our moon-risen collarbones,
the soft lightning
from our fingertips,
and the perfectly soothing sound
of chanted thunder
hiding within our whispered moans.
It is a miracle to say the least,
the way the universe
clings to our human bodies
as they feverishly make love.

It was like watching
the sun set
over an exhausted horizon;
seeing her fall softly
asleep in my arms.

Isn't it an absolutely magical thing
how magnificent and grand
and diverse this world is,
yet we can meet our significant
other in a coffee shop
or bookstore or bar?
How incredibly lovely is this?
Doesn't it just make you want to
get up each faithful morning,
put on your favorite attire,
spin the fitting jazz record,
and walk out your door with
the exquisite hope
that your love
may be waiting for you through
some glass window reading
some book dreaming of
romance
and the color lavender
and the sacred skin
of some other?

We wait for this our entire lives.
What a day to be alive.

We are
the scientists,
trying to make sense
of the stars
inside us.

Today I contemplate my tenderness,
how much of it is left,
if it went away softly into the night
or if I have become an artist
at suppressing it.
I think I choose to be tender
because tender does not ask questions.
There is no doubt in being tender.
One is simply tender because it is natural.
Grandmother with her apron on smiling,
stirring softly her special soup.
Mother's long fingernails sliding slowly
across the small of my back.
Every day I think of different ways to be tender,
as if it is an art form and I can shape it
into what I desire. So I do,
and I will continue to.
Without my tenderness I am without love.
Without love I am without everything.

The purpose of life
isn't just to
be happy.
The purpose of life,
my love,
is to feel.
You must understand
that your pain
is essential.

I have never blended in with
masculine proud men,
if I am honest.
With them it's always,
"You don't have the balls."
I have always been
far too sensitive for that.
With me it's always been,
"You don't have the heart."

You ask me
how I love you,

and the reply
will always remain
the same.

In the spaces
between
seconds.

Last week I found out what true, unconditional love really is.
I watched my grandmother stretched on all fours on the floor
searching desperately through her home for a tiny ruby that
fell off the ring Grandfather gave her. I watched her, thinking
how there was no way she would ever find it, but hoping she did.
She said it could be anywhere. I asked her for an extra flashlight,
and we both searched for hours. I listened to her weep and weep,
and not say a word the entire time. It was contagious.
I thought of when Grandfather gave it to her, what he was thinking,
what she was thinking, if he from above in some other dimension
was watching her, searching faithfully for that ruby as if it would
bring him back. It was in these moments that I realized what I want
from this world, no matter how often the tough, gritty boy
in me likes to hide it; I want to be loved like this. I want to love like this.
I want it to hurt and rise and spill and tremble across my skin.
But in the end, I want to be left with it. That love staring at me
like a tiny ruby gleaming for my eyes from the floor.
I don't care how much it hurts anymore. I want to fall in love,
and never be sorry.

Agape

The thing they are not telling us
is that every minute of every day
we have a choice,
a daring, darling choice
to be the human we wish to be,
to do the things we have always
wanted to do,
to create the art that aches inside us,
every day, a choice.
I hope today,
as the sun rises from its temporary tomb,
we choose to love beyond measure,
without the hollow heat of labels,
without judgment, without selfishness,
without pause.
It is in love we find ourselves
staring back at us, a noble grin,
realizing all that we could be
and all that we are.
And my god, are we beautiful.

There
is absolutely
nothing in this world
more irresistible
than a person
who inspires
by simply
wearing their heart
on
their sleeve.

It will always be the little
details that are telling
of your magic.
The way you walk.
The way you talk.
The way you treat certain people.
The books you read.
The music you listen to.
The way your body responds
to that very music.
Your soul is hidden like
little crystals
in your mannerisms,
your energy,
and the light you sling
upon the world.
Remember this always.
People are watching.

To write something that truly matters
is all I aim for. Something that matters
not only to me but to the congregation.
I want to shape lives and souls into blissful
motion, spilling love and tenderness along
the way as if they were blood, as if they were
the only things keeping me here, as if I
moved only to the sound of them, spoke
only when they rose from their higher throne
and demanded me to have a say.
I wish to change the world one spirit
at a time, starting with myself.
When I look in the mirror, I want my face
to look like a revolution. Gardens should be blood
and blood should be a garden.
When my life is finished, like a warrior
removing his faithful breastplate, I want to look
at everything behind me, everything
I have created, the halo of manifesto
hovering above me, and be proud of what my hands
have done, the energy in which my spirit
has chosen to love. I will not sing a regretful song.
No matter how often my darkness rises
in an attempt at triumph and protests.

I have
a difficult time
balancing letting people
be
who they are
and standing up for
what I believe.

Does it make us
weak
or rather just human
that we run away
from the things we
love the most the
moment they
begin
to hurt us?

Perhaps in
the end
these temporary
fixes
are all we had all
along.

Compassion
is not limited
to loving only what
you understand.
If we are kind
to only what makes us
comfortable,
what then?
Real love is raw,
sometimes it doesn't sleep,
it weeps alone
in corners,
curses the stars
for being unfair.
Real love
stomachs both
the pleasure and pain
of another person.
It's not always
"good vibes only."
I have always hated
that phrase.
Sometimes,
and quite often, I might add,
to love is to be willing
to get dirty.

There is nothing
more awful in this crumbling,
romantic world
than losing something
you love
and knowing
it will never make
its way
back again.

I have always thought that women
can bear more pain than men.
Always have, always will.
I look to my mother, to my grandmother,
the most fierce women—humans—
I have ever known.
Lionhearted and gentle,
able to carry the weight
of a thousand mourning sons.
I do not know how they do it,
for the life of me.
I would be slaughtered already
if asked to carry what they have carried.
So I raise this glass to the mothers,
to the grandmothers,
to the strong women out there soon
to be doing the raising and carrying
of all the weight there is to come;
cheers.
Cheers to all that you are
and all that you do.
Cheers to love and strength.
Cheers to the blues.

I believe
spontaneous kindness
is more
powerful
than their gun.

What is it about this life in the cold truth
that we are destined to feel more than we
can sometimes bear, that anxiety would turn
into this constant, ever-swaying beam,
and we will someday lose the people we love
the very most, and there is nothing,
not a single thing we can do to stop that.
What is it about this life that keeps some
of the best people flirting with suicide,
their ashen knees buckling, their mouths
soft with silence? What is it that sends me
to my typewriter after a day of faithful sadness,
my soul in absolute tears, trying to understand
the beauty in every man, woman, and animal?
I am not sure and I don't know if I will ever be,
but I am learning to look at the miracles,
all of them tall in my existence, miracles
such as the solemn sounds of nature, birds
humming and chirping, chirping and humming,
or the way it feels to remove all pride and
ego and dance with naked rib cage out in the rain,
my body one with cloud and thunder,
or the way it feels to look into the soul eye
of a lover, their spirit tangled with yours,
knowing that if anything is worth it,
anything at all, then it must be this,
it must be this. Perhaps it is only this,
and everything else creeps quietly
like hooded bravado in the shadows.

Why is it that
society has taught
the human race
to stare at people
with their eyes rather
than their souls?

In all you do,
absolutely everything,
may love be the core,
may love be the essence.

All I want,
all I've ever wanted,
since the bones in me
began to grow
with the flowers,
is to know love,
and for love, too,
to know me.

It was rather beautiful,
the way he put her insecurities
to sleep.
The way he dove
into her eyes
and starved all the fears
and tasted all the dreams
she kept coiled
beneath her bones.

I want nothing more
than to simply
climb the curvature
of your existence,
making a home there,
my body;
to love
and to be loved.

I will love you,
not starting with
your skin or your
organs or your
bones;
I will love madly first
your naked soul.

What I hope
will define
a human
when his life
has ended
and his soul has
sailed away
to become one
with the universe
is what he did
with the love
that was born
in his skull.

the greatest ecstasy
lies in the first graze
of a magic thing
you thought
you'd never touch.

I hope you fall in love with
the journey and not just the idea
of the destination. I hope every day,
every single day of your waking life,
that you choose to do the things
that illuminate the world around you,
things that keep a fresh smile spilled
across your face and thunderous laughter
in your belly. I hope you kiss your friends
in public and tell them in strange, unique ways
that you love them. Send them quirky postcards.
Buy them exotic flowers. I hope you find peace
in good art, good music, compassion, intimacy,
and goodness. I hope you find new and inventive
ways to love yourself and to keep falling in love
with yourself no matter how hard things get,
and I hope you feverishly inspire others
to do the same. I hope, truly hope,
and please know that I believe in you
just as I believe that I exist in this moment
right now, writing this letter of hope to you.
And if by chance someone asks you,
their eyes doubtful and tired,
"What good is hope?"
I hope you'll reply with these words:
"Ah, well, hope, sweet hope,
is all that I know."

The strongest, most
brave people
are the people
who give everything away
without hesitation,
with a stomach full of love,
never, ever expecting
a single thing
in return.

I want to fall in love
with someone's spirit.
Not what they look like,
or what they do.
I want to fall in love
with simply who they are
every minute of every day.
I want essence.

Your sensitivity is your armor,
my friend,
and don't let anyone
tell you different.
It may be both
a blessing and a curse
to be this way,
to inhale all that performs
around you,
but at the end of the day
it is an absolute privilege
to be gentle,
an honor to truly care
about the things most people miss.

To you, a pebble is a cathedral.
To you, a grain of sand
has a beating heart.

This is why you matter in this world.
We need more eyes like yours.

Every day is such a new thing.
Delicious in all of its colors.
Whomever I want to be, I am.
Wherever I want to go, I go.
Whatever name I wish to carry, I do.
If I want to weep, I weep.
If I want to sing, I sing.
Every day is such a new thing.
I wake up with a woman sleeping
next to me,
her lavender hair draped
over my shoulders like a silk curtain,
poetry sprouts from the silence
of her sleeping, her dreaming,
I read it to myself,
over and over again
until I believe it, and I do.
You have not lived until you
turn on a jazz record,
lie down with your woman,
move your fingertips
strategically from her shoulders
down to the small of her back,
all the while the jazz
filling the room,
the piano disguised as love,
the sax as truth,
the drums passion,
it's all here,
in this bed,
on the sacred spin
of this timeless,
new woman.

I drank her silence like liquor,
and it destroyed me the same,
but I fell for all of her,
hopelessly and endlessly.
My soul will always be lifted
when she walks into the room,
and my blood will always dance
when her breath passes through me.

Some of my favorite
seconds on Earth are
the seconds filled with
my lips spilled
upon your collarbone
and my hair nestled into
your fist.

there's something
so very sacred in every sound
that has ever took me;
a church bell ringing,
a solo saxophone,
a quiet man's shuffling hands
beneath a table,
a child's laughter springing
like a lily from his mother's yard.
these sounds,
all of them,
save me every single day,
my quiet mouth a zipper,
my heart an amethyst stone
in the quivering hands
of a grieving mother.
I can't stop hearing the music;
I never want to.
I am so happy here
on my throne of observation,
watching other people exist,
their flickers,
their smiles,
their quirky ecstasies.
If a sweet woman or man
never finds me
in the way I wish,
rich with unconditional,
unconventional love,
I shall be happy to die
right here in the arms
of Earth.

I will go gladly.
Humanity; my lover.

Seeing the best in people,
the bruised, mosaic light stretching
for a way out of the cracks,
is the greatest, most burdensome
art I have ever known.

There
was a reason
she was so
romantic
about the moon.
It never asked her
questions or
begged for the answers,
nor did she
ever have
to prove herself to it.
It was always just there—
breathing, shining,
and in ways most humans
can't understand;
listening.

I can love things
simply by watching her
love them—
that is how
I know I love her.

There is always
a lovely way
to look at things,
you know?
Like the days we
spend apart
are as beautiful
and essential
as the spaces between
the stars.

In the end
I would rather be
able to say
I loved too much
than not enough.

The blessing
and the curse:
continuing,
over and over again,
to always see
the best in people,
no matter the cost.

It is the little things with you,
from every small detail,
every fraction that makes you up entirely.
I must express my love,
confess it from where I stand, and
tell you my wish is to never be
without you.
To never be apart.
I find so much magic placed
strategically on your skin,
from beauty marks, to freckles,
to the way your bones and skin
seem to be in perfect conversation
with each other,
the magic, always there.
You are never without it.
I want to fall asleep with you
and wake up to you.
I want to hear you speak about
your day, your longings,
your aches.
I want to listen to the way you
fall asleep and fall into
my own slumber because of it.
I want you. Today. Tomorrow.
And for the years to come.
My knees are bowed
and my heart open.
I, am yours.

I will love you
with the sea
and you must believe
that I will die
with nothing but salt
in my bones.

What you love
you must love
with the entirety
of your soul.

Every human being on this planet
is battling something, so for the life
of me I will never understand why we
are so cruel to one another, why we
do not love often and more naturally,
and why sympathy toward our fellow human
has become such a mystical thing.
Where are our eyes, our spirits,
our blood pumping and beating hearts
when they are needed most?
The formula, when we get down to the
bone of it, is simple. Be gentle. Be kind.
Treat every living soul with the tenderness
of a mother. Be forgiving and hold no grudges.
We speak of love like it is this mundane,
cliché reference, but at the end of it all,
when we throw in the towel, the white flag
raised high and holy to the cosmos,
love will be the only thing left.
The only thing that truly mattered.
Our only purpose is to invest in it.
To treat it like music, moving our bodies
to it, our eyes wide and our hearts
open in relentless bloom.

Philautia

Here's to the empaths.
To the emotional artists.
To the ones whose outlet
is simply feeling.
You are braver than
you know.

Every morning I court
self-love down to the water,
dipping its warm body and blood
like a cup,
"This is your baptism,"
I say,
"This is how you move
from brokenness to triumph,
from dependency to grace."

It is safe to say
that every day I am learning,
building a home
within me
that I am not afraid
to walk into.

Each day
I find myself getting
one more step into the door,
more prepared,
more ready,
and I know a day will come,
some day very soon,
when I will crawl
my tired legs
up that wondrous staircase,
see my bed sitting there
spirit-like in my room,
and I will run to it like a child,
jump into the white, snowy sheets,
and closing my eyes unfurling
an inevitable smile,
I will touch myself like a lover
and whisper into my own being,
"This is the secret.
The secret to everything."

There are many men in me,
and how truly often I war with each
one of them, bouncing between them
like a swift rabbit hungry for some place
to call home. The men, both masculine
and feminine, like to whisper sweet nothings
to my third eye: "You're too sweet for this
cruel world," they say. "You're too weak
to hold all of the suffering you see and feel,
too weak, and you'll always be."
And I am afraid I have become
much too comfortable listening to them.
Yet the pure boy in me is hungry;
his eyes are wide and filled with
perfect passion, his stance that of
a virtuoso who walks in shy valleys
with spontaneous tempo.
I am ready. Whoever the *I* is;
he, she, they, are ready.
I have spent too many nights beneath
the luscious stars in cold confusion.

I have wept too many tears that
were never my own.
I have fucked for the sake of fucking
when making love was a myriad memory
stuck in the back of my throat.
I am searching for the man in me
that wakes up every morning,
starts a pot of coffee, returns
to the bathroom to wash his face
and with one look in the mirror
sees a dream, a poem, a revolution.
He sees the person he wants
to spend the rest of his life with.

The romantic thing
about the darkness
was always
the constant pull
toward the light.

How exhaustingly
heavy it becomes
romanticizing
too much
too often
and at the end of the day
still remaining
without love.

No faces. No color.
No hue of judgment.
Written across the body
and soul of every being
is something that urges me
to just love, love, love;
human. Simply human,
we all are, indeed.

I am the dark
and I am the light.
I am the moon
and the starless
night sky.
Fall in love with all
that I am
or do not fall in love
with me at all.

true intimacy
is the quiet fire
I feel
when I kiss you
in places
the sun
never touches.

lately I have been
drinking tequila—
1800 Silver—as a way
to reincarnate
a different decade
my grandparents
lived in
when the bartenders
raised their hot fists
at drunkards
and Victorian mirrors
hung like trippy stars
on bathroom walls
this has been my
agenda slipping briskly
into the skin
of others before me
romanticizing the past
with fever and passion
so much so that last
week I went out
and bought a teal suit

put a flower
in the left-hand pocket
and walked
the sleepless city
listening to slow jazz
pretending to be
my grandfather
heading to a dive bar
where he would meet
June
a woman of intense
spiritual gleam
and sensitivity
and kindness
a woman whom I
with white light
in my eyes
would one day
crown as my
grandmother.

It's not that
I do not want beauty;
that has
never been the dilemma.
It's that I fear
there is so very much
of it,
all around me,
in every person
and thing,
I am not sure
my sensitive heart
will be able to bear it.

the tiring labels
of *masculine*
and *feminine*
and their separation
diminishes
the free-flow individual
freedom of expression
I believe we have so much more
inside us than we will ever know
both masculine and feminine
we're all so afraid
afraid to be different
in the wrong way
afraid to be falsely labeled
afraid to be harshly dissected
afraid to not be enough
but most of all
and perhaps it's just me
afraid. so intensely afraid
to not be interesting.

inhale.
exhale.
I will love,
with the entire
cosmos inside me.

trust your blooming
earth child.
breathe slowly
and receive patience.
you are worth
only what you allow
yourself to be.

you know what
truly aches
all that you are?
having so much
inside you
but not having
the slightest clue
how to pour it out.

When I became
old enough
to understand my tears,
I fell in love with them.
The way they made me
feel sad, and at the same time,
beautiful.
I do not fear
my tears.
I fear becoming so numb
one day
that they will no longer
be able to fall.

I want
to marry,
each
and every day,
each second
I am with you.

It is no mystery
that those who endure
the most pain
are the strongest people
on this planet.
When hardship
comes early,
it molds us,
the pain thickens
our bones,
our marrow golden plated
and lion tough.
I ask of every one of you,
including myself,
may we always stay strong,
through the loss of love
and family,
through sorrow and depression,
through the waves of imbalance,
through everything.
May we lean on each other,
our shoulders a pillow
for our brothers,
our sisters,
our strangers,
our animals.
We are all in this together.
Whether we choose
to believe that or not.

Sometimes
I am terrified
of my intense hunger
to live,
because dying
has always seemed
like the easier option.

I have
not fallen in love
with a body,
but merely
a soul,
and that
has made
all the difference.

Above all, know that you are not alone
in your suffering, whatever it may be.
This life throws stones at us, casts them
from every direction with fantastic rhythm,
and sometimes it feels as if we cannot stop them,
as if it is just a part of life, and I suppose it is.
I see the scars on every man, every woman,
the sheer tiredness in their eyes. So many of us,
tired. That is why I will never understand why people
are so cruel to one another; we all bleed the same color,
drink from Earth's waters, share the same cosmos.
If only we saw this more often, looked past the labels
and first impressions and judgment. If only, if only.
Could you imagine the world we would exist in?
Everyone's hands fit into one another's,
locked tightly like flower petals pressed firmly
into the worn pages of a book.

On that day
I grew
to understand
my Gemini blood—
I feel so much
sometimes
to the point
of feeling nothing
at all.

I love us
for the way
our eyes
make love
to each other's
souls.

after all, we
are made of
earth
and even it
goes through
seasons.

above all,
treat each
human being
with complete delicacy.
true therapy
exists inside
the spirit
of simple kindness.

love
in such a way
that it haunts
the hate in others.

My entire life
I have felt as if I were onstage,
performing my feminine mannerisms
and characteristics
to the people around me,
the spontaneous crowd,
family, friends, lovers.
I feel this mountainous need
to perform something
with natural charisma,
something I am not quite sure of yet,
but I always know it when I feel it.
Say in some random pub in a new city
reciting Rimbaud to the bartender;
or in Central Park carrying a copy
of *Howl,* frolicking along to the sound
of birds as if they were little winged
instruments just flapping their winded
sounds around;
or say in a bed with a new lover,
her pale skin soft in midnight matrimony,
running my fingers strategically
down her spine as if she
were a grand piano dimly lit
to speak sonnets to the crowd.
I always feel as if I am surrounded
by lights beaming down, begging
for my body.
I want someone to look at me
and instantly feel the spirit of jazz.

Know that I love you,
that I have always loved you,
in ways that go without saying,
in seasons that tease
you to give up,
at your worst,
at my worst,
I love you,
I have never needed a reason.
Simply your existence
is reason enough.

Some people
just aren't meant for
this world.
They see too much
and feel too much
far too early
and we try to fix them
and tell them
it will be okay
but it never will.

To me
these are the angels.

The misunderstood.

To be
socially awkward
isn't a flaw.
Society tries
to tell us
otherwise.
I go out
and see so many
plastic faces,
hear so much lukewarm
bullshit.
Anytime I see
a quiet person,
I think to myself,
"Ah, beautiful.
So you understand."

In her arms of
ecstasy
and her eyes
of fire
I belong
to no one
but her.

In our oneness
I am aroused.

I will forever
be a hopeful
romantic,
and not just
with people
but with places,
things,
songs,
animals.
I place my love
into everything electric
and soft,
leaving my heart open
like a rose
to the beauty.

Physical beauty
may seem like
it controls the world
but the soul
and spirit
sustain
and heal it.

I see so very many people
wearing "I don't give a damn,"
like a medal.
And that's quite all right;
it's good to not give a damn
about some things.
But too often they use it
as an excuse,
an excuse not to care
about the noble things.
Give me someone who
gives a damn about
what truly matters—
nature, cosmos, animals,
climate change,
nurturing humanity,
bettering mental illness,
our youth.
And the list goes on.
It takes more strength
to give a damn
than to not.

I just want to be around people
who care.

At the heart of it,
we all just want purpose.
Something sacred.
A reason to wake up
each noble morning,
roll over,
and feel the soft dream
of passion,
a lover sleeping next
to us,
promise like lifting incense
in the air.

we want truth
and freedom
and love.

we want to be heard.

A good poem can fix
just about every wound in me,
my blood buried and covered
in the tall valleys of verse,
my energy drenched
in the diction of chord
between each letter.
Because of poetry
I am brave,
tough, able to accept
bullets pressing into my skin.
I live in this house,
this house with faithful lines
and linen,
lines like,
"When I am naked
I feel like my own god,"
or,
"The truth is a moon
buried beneath centuries
of sadness."
Poetry is a way out
and a way in.
A way out of meaninglessness
and pride and ego and hate.
A way in of truth and self
and enlightenment and beauty.
When asked why I love poetry
I will pause for a brief moment,
flip my hair to one side,
and whisper a reply
of confidence,
"Because every moment
I have wished to die,
poetry has assured me
that is not an option."

Simply
touching you
is poetry
enough.

When they ask me
on my deathbed
what the purpose
of life is,
what it was for me,
I will turn my eyes
to them,
shed a natural grin,
and reply the only way
I know how,
"To love her,
and to do so in a way
that even through death
she will never
be without me."

My entire life
I have been told
I don't listen,
my eyes staring
starry-eyed
off into space,
into oblivion.
Every time, my reply
is the same—
"Why of course I do.
Just not to the same things
you do."

Last night I dreamt of seven different
angels who symbolized seven different lives
I have already lived. One of them named Afriel.
One Ariel. One Cassiel. One Charmeine.
One Dina. One Gavreel. One Michael.
Each one I loved madly.
In my first life I was a forever child,
I lived one hundred years,
danced through my days with gypsy grace
and never let the sadness of the world
steal my yearning to soar. And soar I did.
In my second life I had the eyes of ocean,
my veins were roots to the tree of life,
I slept outside in quiet unison,
the cosmos drugged me into a lucid state,
the oblivion nearly fucked me blind.
And I loved it.
In my third life I studied temperance;
my bones learned to be as patient
as the birth of day.
I treated my beautiful body
like a temple, and slept silently
on my mother's howling grave.
In my fourth life I lived in tune with Earth's cry,
the birds and the sea and the spiritual
harmony of big cities.
My soul was pure music and everyone heard it.
In my fifth life I was a professor of poetry.
I spoke in sonnets and chords and lovers
told me my lips tasted like honey.
I never believed them until I had a dream
where I made love to God.

In my sixth life I was a revolutionary for peace.
I brought people together with the sound of music,
and every night we chased the roaring thunder
of the almighty sea.
In my seventh life I loved one woman
until death do us part.
We ran wildly through meadows
and carved our ancient names
into the noble, neon sky.
The entire world was ours.

Andrews McMeel Publishing
a division of Andrews McMeel Universal
1130 Walnut Street, Kansas City, Missouri 64106

www.andrewsmcmeel.com

18 19 20 21 22 BVG 10 9 8 7 6 5 4 3 2 1

ISBN: 978-1-4494-9677-7

Library of Congress Control Number: 2018949447

Editor: Patty Rice
Designer/Art Director: Julie Barnes
Production Editor: Elizabeth A. Garcia
Production Manager: Cliff Koehler
Cover art: Janice Rago